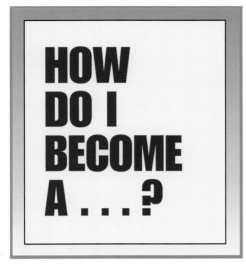

HOW DO I BECOME A . . . ?

POLICE OFFICER

Mindi Rose Englart

Photographs by Peter Casolino

BLACKBIRCH®
PRESS

THOMSON
—★—
GALE

San Diego • Detroit • New York • San Francisco • Cleveland • New Haven, Conn. • Waterville, Maine • London • Munich

THOMSON

GALE

© 2002 by Blackbirch Press™. Blackbirch Press™ is an imprint of The Gale Group, Inc., a division of Thomson Learning, Inc.

Blackbirch Press™ and Thomson Learning™ are trademarks used herein under license.

For more information, contact
The Gale Group, Inc.
27500 Drake Rd.
Farmington Hills, MI 48331-3535
Or you can visit our Internet site at http://www.gale.com

Photo Credits: Cover, all photos © Peter Casolino

LIBRARY OF CONGRESS CATALOGING-IN-PUBLICATION DATA

Englart, Mindi.
  police officer / by Mindi Rose Englart.
    v. cm. — (How do I become a: series)
  Includes index.
  Contents: Policing today — How to become a police officer — Police academy — Swearing in — Roll call — 911: call for help — Inside the police car — The uniform — Investigative services — Making an arrest — Records department — Forensics — Community policing — The police chief — Partnership with the community — Motorcycle unit — Animal control — Spanky the police dog — Mounted police.
  ISBN 1-56711-417-2
  1. Police—Juvenile literature. 2. Law enforcement—Vocational guidance—Juvenile literature. [1. Police—Vocational guidance. 2. Vocational guidance.]
  I. Title. II. Series.
  HV7922 .E54 2003
  363.2—dc21   2002003949

Printed in China
10 9 8 7 6 5 4 3 2 1

Contents

Dedication
To my dad, Alan Englart

Special Thanks
The publisher and the author would like to thank Chief Melvin H. Wearing, Judy Mongillo, and the New Haven Police Department for their generous help in putting this project together.

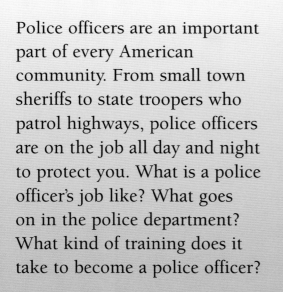

Police officers are an important part of every American community. From small town sheriffs to state troopers who patrol highways, police officers are on the job all day and night to protect you. What is a police officer's job like? What goes on in the police department? What kind of training does it take to become a police officer?

Police officers help keep communities safe. ▶

An officer in his police car

Policing Today

There are more than 600,000 police officers in the United States today. There are three basic types of police departments:

- town and city departments
- sheriffs' departments
- state police departments

Sheriffs' departments police rural areas, and state police departments provide police service to all areas of a state not served by a sheriff or town police department. State police also often patrol the highways of a state.

New York City has the largest police department in the United States with about 39,500 officers.

An officer puts
on his uniform. ▶

▼ A New Haven police officer looks
at the day's information.

The New Haven Police Department (NHPD), in New Haven, Connecticut, has 472 police officers who serve about 125,000 citizens. Another 180 people who are not police officers also work in the NHPD. The police department needs secretaries, file clerks, and other office workers to help officers carry out their duties.

5

How to Become a Police Officer

To become a police officer in the United States, a person must train at a special school called a police academy. People who want to attend a police academy have to meet certain requirements. They must be American citizens. They must also be old enough to apply—each state has its own minimum age requirement. They cannot have a criminal record, and they must live in or near the town where they will work. Some police academies only admit students who already have a college degree.

People who meet all of these requirements then take a written test, called a civil service test, which all government employees must take. They also do weight lifting, sit-ups, and a 1.5-mile run as part of a standard physical fitness test. People who pass these tests are then interviewed. They are asked questions to make sure they are right for academy training. Finally, they have a medical exam and take a drug test. After they pass all of these tests, they may be accepted into the police academy.

Taking the civil service test ▼

Police Academy

Most academies provide a six-month training program. The program teaches students about the Constitution and the legal system.

A big part of police academy training takes place in the classroom. ▶

Students also learn lifesaving and self-defense techniques, and how to use weapons to protect people. Students receive weapons training that includes target practice and the safe handling of guns. They also learn to use pepper spray and the PR24, or nightstick, which is a stick with a handle. Police officers always try to resolve problems without the use of force. They use weapons rarely and only to protect themselves or others.

New Haven Police Academy students volunteer at soup kitchens, homeless shelters, and health clinics to help them better understand the residents they will serve.

◄ **Students use guns loaded with paint pellets during weapons training.**

For example, if a student has a class about homelessness, he or she may spend a night sleeping in a homeless shelter to see what it is like.

Police academy students take psychology classes to help them understand why people think and behave in certain ways. Students also act out situations they may face on the job, such as making an arrest.

▲ **Students are trained to use their radios.**

9

▲ **Police academy physical training**

Students receive physical training and work on communication skills so they can resolve problems without the use of force. They also learn about the police department's procedures. For example, they are taught how to handle evidence carefully and how to make traffic stops.

A class does push-ups. ▶

Swearing In

After students have completed police academy training, they have a graduation and swearing-in ceremony. At the swearing in, new officers recite the *Law Enforcement Code of Ethics*. With this pledge, the officers promise to enforce the law, to serve and protect all citizens, and to help keep property safe. Officers also promise to respect the constitutional rights of all people, to be honest, and to set a good example for others.

After they graduate from the police academy, students go into a six- to eight-week-long training program. This program pairs new graduates with experienced officers who act as on-the-job instructors. The new officers, or rookies, watch the experienced officers at work. They do not perform their police duties until they feel comfortable in their jobs.

▲ **An officer swears in.**

11

Roll Call

Police officers usually work eight hours in a row. This is called a shift. At the beginning of each shift, a police supervisor takes attendance, or roll call. The captain makes sure all of the officers that are scheduled for the shift have arrived. Then he or she lets them know what to watch out for on the shift. For example, a captain may announce a bank robbery that happened earlier in the day. He or she gives a description of the robber and hands out a picture that was taken from the bank's security camera. That way, the officers know how to look for the robber.

◀ **Officers line up for roll call and take notes.**

▲ Police dispatchers must have a great deal of patience.

911: Call for Help

Police officers are trained to help people. People who need help may call the emergency help line, 911. If a 911 caller requires help from the police, the call is forwarded to the Central Complaint Service (CCS) at the police department. Here, a dispatcher assistant takes down information about the problem. The assistant then enters this information into a computer system. Once the information has been entered into the computer, the police dispatcher takes over.

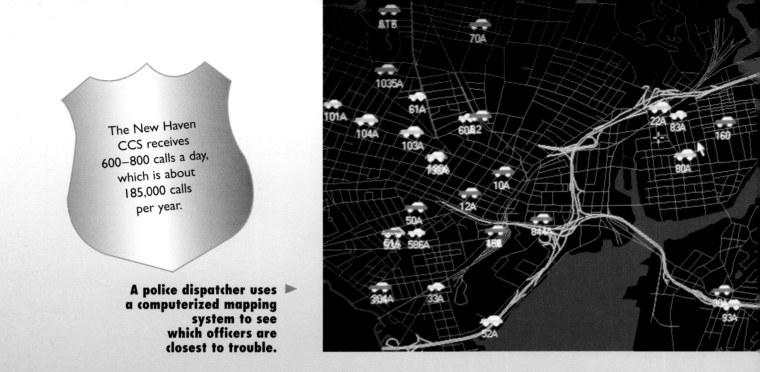

A police dispatcher uses a computerized mapping system to see which officers are closest to trouble. ▶

The police dispatcher is responsible for sending officers to the scene of an emergency. Police dispatchers need to remain calm under pressure, so they receive special training to improve their communication skills. They must be able to give and get important information quickly. They are also trained on a computer system that allows them to see where police cars are located at all times.

Calls to 911 are handled according to how urgent they are. If a call is not urgent, information can be sent over radio or by a Mobile Data Terminal (MDT). Information sent by MDT shows up on a laptop computer in a police car. If a call is urgent—such as when a crime is in progress—the police dispatcher quickly sends a radio message to all officers. The radio message tells the officers who are closest to the crime to go to the scene right away.

Inside the Police Car

A police car is like any other car except for a few important things. Police cars have special lights and sirens that officers use in emergencies to alert drivers that they are in a hurry. When drivers see or hear a police car's lights and siren, they are supposed to move to the side of the road to allow the police car to pass them easily. This helps police get to crime scenes as quickly as possible.

Police cars need to be in good shape, and they have certain special features because officers drive a lot. Police cars have heavy-duty shock absorbing systems, sturdy tires, and fast engines. These features make the police car ride smoother, and drive safer and faster than regular cars. Sometimes police officers even use their cars to chase criminals!

Many cities have laptop computers in their police cars. This allows the police dispatcher to send information to officers by e-mail. Officers can even receive a photo of a person police think may have committed a crime, called a suspect, on their MDTs.

An officer looks at information sent on his MDT. ▶

The Uniform

Police officers wear badges, nameplates, patches, and pins on their uniforms so people can identify them. Police uniforms also help people tell the difference between a state trooper and a local police officer. Patches on their uniforms show what town officers work for. Numbered badges, pins, and other patches show an officer's rank, or position. Police officers can hold the rank of patrol officer, detective, sergeant, lieutenant, captain, assistant chief, or chief. Officers also wear pins to show that they are part of a special unit, such as a motorcycle unit.

◄ **One of the most important items an officer carries is a radio.**

One of the most important parts of a police uniform is the belt. Officers keep many items on their belts, like pepper spray, a gun, extra bullets, a nightstick, handcuffs, rubber gloves, and a flashlight.

Officers also carry a handheld radio and a pager, so that they can be in constant contact with headquarters. Many officers wear a bulletproof vest under their shirts. Bulletproof vests are made of special fibers that do not allow bullets to pass through them. A bulletproof vest can save an officer's life.

▼ **A PR24 (nightstick)**

▲ **Handcuffs**

17

Detectives

Detectives are police officers who are a rank above patrol officers. Patrol officers are usually called to a crime scene first. If they determine that further investigation is necessary, officers will turn the case over to detectives to investigate.

An officer must pass some written tests to become a detective, but no special training is required. Detectives share information with other city, state, and federal law enforcement agencies. They help to solve all kinds of crimes, including robbery, burglary, and murder.

Detectives sometimes have to get suspects' trust to get information from them about a crime. This can be difficult for uniformed police officers, because when criminals see their uniforms, they may hide or not talk about certain things. Detectives do not wear uniforms, so it is possible for them to work undercover, or without letting the suspect know they are police officers. This can help the detective to discover evidence that uniformed officers might not be able to find.

◁ **A plainclothes officer makes an arrest.**

A forensic detective brushes a glass dish for fingerprints.

INKED PALM PRINT

1
2
3
4
5

Forensic Detectives

When a case goes to court, forensic, or medical, evidence may be used to prove that a crime was committed. Forensic detectives learn to gather, study, and prepare evidence found at crime scenes, for use in court if necessary. They must take classes in photography so that they know how to photograph the important parts of a crime scene. Forensic detectives are trained to notice small details that may provide clues to a crime.

Forensic detectives like to solve mysteries. An important part of their job is to collect and study fingerprints. Since each person's fingerprints are unique, this kind of evidence can help police connect a criminal to a crime. Forensic detectives often provide clues in robbery and murder cases.

As scientists make new discoveries, forensic detectives gain new ways to collect criminal evidence. Today, forensic detectives use genetic science. Genetics is a form of biology that deals with the unique features of a person. Just like all people have unique fingerprints, they also have a unique DNA, or genetic make-up. From a hair or nail sample, a forensic detective can gather DNA information that can help prove whether a person was involved in a crime.

What makes a good fingerprint? One thing is sweat— it helps to transfer a fingerprint onto an object.

Using a magnifying glass to see fingerprints ▷

Making an Arrest

If officers have good reason, called probable cause, to believe a crime was committed, they can investigate. Before police officers arrest suspects, they must read them their rights, called Miranda rights. Police officers must make sure that suspects understand that they do not have to answer any questions without a lawyer present to help them. To protect people's constitutional rights, officers may have to get permission from a judge, called a search warrant, before they can search suspects or their property.

◀ **Officers handcuff and detain a suspect.**

When suspects are arrested, they are handcuffed and brought to a detention center, or jail. There, an officer takes information about the suspect. Then the officer takes the suspect's fingerprints and an arrest photo. This information and photo are kept on file in the records department. Soon after suspects are put in jail, a judge tells them how much money it will cost to get out until their trial starts. This is called setting a bail. If suspects pay their bail, they can go home until their assigned trial date. If they cannot pay bail, they must stay in jail.

23

Records Department

Whenever a person is arrested, a file is created and kept in the police records department. A person can have a file for any kind of offense, from damaging property to murder. Local, state, and federal records departments can share files on suspects to help identify and locate them.

In New Haven, the records department is managed by a police officer, called the keeper of records. This officer supervises 40 people, called record clerks. Over 100,000 criminal records are on file in New Haven. Copies of these records can be sent to MDTs in police cars to help officers identify a wanted criminal.

There are over 100,000 files in the NHPD records department. ▼

The police chief has a lot of responsibility.

The Police Chief

A police chief is the head of the entire police department. He or she has a lot of responsibility. Police chiefs are in charge of all of the officers in their department. They also work with community leaders and citizens to stay informed about what is going on in their city. The police chief is on call 24 hours a day, seven days a week. If there is a serious situation, such as a hostage crisis, the chief is likely to be on the scene.

Chief Melvin H. Wearing became New Haven's first African American police chief in 1997. Chief Wearing never expected to become a police chief when he began his career as a police officer in 1968. He and the NHPD have won many awards for their high quality police service.

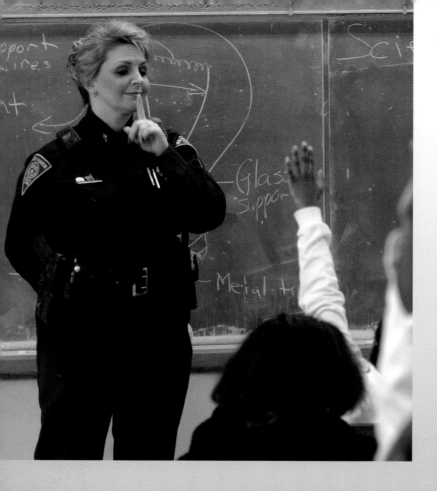

Officer Hollie Miller talks to school kids about safety issues.

Partnership with the Community

Police officers participate in their communities in many ways. For example, some are school resource officers whose job is to keep students safe in school. Officers may also go into schools to educate children about drug and violence prevention, or gun safety.

The Police Athletic League (PAL) can be found in many American communities. In the PAL program, police officers volunteer their time to teach young boys and girls about sports or recreational activities, such as street hockey, chess, and cheerleading. The program seeks to show kids that cops are people too—that they are there to help, that they care about their communities.

The police department also works closely with many local social service agencies. Social service agencies help people when they have problems. Officers make sure people who need emergency housing, food, or medical attention are put in touch with the right agencies.

Motorcycle Unit

The main job of a motorcycle officer is to keep roads safe. This is an important responsibility because motor vehicle accidents are one of the leading causes of death in America. Many of these officers know how to ride motorcycles before they join the police force, but they still need special training. They must learn how to handle their motorcycles while they do police work. Like other traffic officers, those in the motorcycle unit also learn to use radar equipment to tell how fast a vehicle is traveling.

Motorcycle officers are assigned to areas that have a high rate of traffic violations. These officers check to make sure that drivers wear seat belts, have not been drinking alcohol, and drive within posted speed limits. Motorcycle officers also help to control crowds at special events, such as parades, concerts, and sports events.

Motorcycle units help to ▶ keep roads safe.

Motorcycle officers are issued cars as well as motorcycles—when the weather is bad, they use cars.

▲ **Officer Ray Crowley and his partner, Spanky.**

K-9 Unit

Officers who work with dogs are in the K-9 unit of the police department. "K-9" sounds like "canine," which is another word for dog. A police dog can be trained to search for people, criminal evidence, explosives, or drugs.

One job within the K-9 unit is an explosive detection canine handler. This means that an officer works with a police dog to find bombs. Officers must complete a special 5-week bomb technician training class to learn how to disarm explosive devices. The dogs' training lasts even longer. They train for 10 weeks, 5 of them with their handlers. By the end of their training, dogs can detect all materials used to make bombs.

Officer Ray Crowley and Spanky check for ▶ explosives at Tweed New Haven airport.

This is a high-risk police job—it's not for everyone! Explosive detection canine handlers must pay close attention to their dogs to pick up on their clues. For example, an officer can tell by the way the dog's tail wags whether it has found explosives or it just smells another animal.

Police dogs are sometimes called search and rescue dogs. These dogs can be trained to search buildings and other areas to catch criminals or to find lost children. Officers and their dogs often become very attached to one another. In fact, police dogs are considered an officer's partner—some dogs even live with their handlers!

Spanky and Officer Ray Crowley have protected many well-known people, such as President George W. Bush.

Mounted Police

Mounted police officers are different from other types of officers because they patrol on horseback. Mounted police add a friendly feel to the areas they patrol. People like to pet the horses and talk with the officers. Mounted police are also used to control crowds during large events, such as sports events or concerts.

Mounted police need to feel comfortable performing their duties on horseback. Though many of these officers have ridden horses all of their lives, both the officers and their horses must attend about eight weeks of training before they begin work. During training, officers learn how to keep their horses healthy. They also learn how to clean stables and how to drive the vehicles that transport their horses. Each officer is assigned one horse. This way, horse and rider get to know each other and can create a trusting relationship.

▲ Kids love to say "hi" to police horses.

Community Policing

Over the last 10 years, more cities and towns have decided to use community policing. Community police officers focus on motor vehicle violations, noise complaints, thefts, graffiti, and drug offenses. A police officer is assigned to a certain neighborhood. The officer talks with people who live and work in that neighborhood, and together they work to solve problems. Since community policing gets more officers on the street, it becomes harder for criminals to commit crimes.

New Haven community police officers also talk with the Board of Young Adult Police Commissioners. This group of high school students meets regularly to tell the local police about neighborhood issues that concern them.

In New Haven, police officers are assigned to regular beats, or areas, in their 10 community policing districts. Each of these districts has a small police station, called a substation. This gives the police and the people in the community a place to meet with each other. As people get to know their local police officers, they become comfortable enough to share information with them. Officers use this information to help them do their jobs better. Community policing has helped reduce crime by 55% in New Haven in the past 10 years! Whether an officer is driving a car or a motorcycle, on a horse, or on foot, they are there to help.

Officer John Burke patrolled this New Haven ▶ neighborhood for 7 years.

Glossary

Community policing Residents and police working together to reduce crime in neighborhoods

Detective An officer who investigates crimes

Enforcement Helping to make sure a law is obeyed

Forensics Using science to solve crimes

Homicide Murder

Law A rule

Suspect A person believed to have committed a crime

For More Information

Official Website of the New Haven Police Department

www.newhavenpolice.org

Index